Entrancing English

Barbara Ruben

In a cave far away, lives a powerful wizard named Whimstaff. He spends his days finding the answers to ancient English problems and has parchments filled with wonderful words. In this book, Whimstaff shares his knowledge to help you to master the art of English.

Whimstaff has a goblin assistant named Pointy, who is very clever. Pointy helps Whimstaff perfect his spells and gets annoyed with the laziness of Mugly and Bugly, his fat pet frogs. They spend most of their time eating and sleeping and do as little work as possible.

Pointy also helps Whimstaff look after Miss Snufflebeam. She is a young dragon who is rather clumsy and often loses Whimstaff's words!

Wizard Whimstaff and his friends are very happy solving English problems. Join them on a magical quest to win the Trophy of English Wizardry!

Contents

Agitating Adjectives

Hello, young apprentice. I'm Wizard Whimstaff and I'm here to teach you about **adjectives**. Good English wizards know that there are always so many wonderful **describing words** to choose from. However, there are some boring words that sloppy wizards use again and again, such as **nice** or **awful**. These words can mean millions of things. For example, look at my wizard's chair.

Instead of saying my chair is nice we could say it was comfortable, soft, grand, restful, snug or even velvety!

Task 1 Have a go at this exercise. Don't worry if it seems hard at first! Replace these words with an adjective that really tells the reader something. Try to picture the objects in your head so that your words are really descriptive! How do they smell, or feel?

Remember to use your dictionary and your thesaurus.

a nice _____ weather

b nice _____ cauldron

c nice _____ time

d nice _____ wand

e nice _____ personality

f nice _____ taste

g nice _____ frog

h nice _____ potions

Task 2 Hey presto! That was excellent work! Now replace the word **awful** with an adjective that really tells the reader something.

a awful wizard _____

b awful chanting _____

c awful spell _____

d awful hat _____

e awful job _____

f awful accident _____

g awful car _____

h awful monster _____

Task 3 Abracadabra! Here are some words I have conjured from my cauldron. Put as many as possible of them into really interesting and descriptive sentences. Don't use any of them more than once. I have done the first one for you.

stinking powerful wild
magical energetic
tragic sparkling lonely
jealous flowing
delicious tuneless

a We had a delicious dragon scale and cucumber sandwich by the banks of the flowing river.

b

c

d

e

f

Sorcerer's Skill Check

Just to make sure that you can use your magic to create wonderful descriptive words, put these words into sentences on a separate sheet of paper.

dull   dingy   glittering   vicious   salty   silky

You are clever! Put your first silver shield on your trophy at the back of the book!

Wonderful Words

I'm Pointy, Wizard Whimstaff's assistant! I have to tell you about **persuasive language**. Advertisements use a lot of persuasive language! That means the words **try to get you to agree** with the views of the person who has written them.

New Formula Stardust with real star glitter!!!

STARDUST

A MUST for every good sorcerer! There's no spell it can't create!

Task 1 Look at this advertisement describing a new broomstick, called the Whizzer. It's full of persuasive language. Can you pick it out and then underline the words? You'll soon get the hang of it!

Be the first on your mountain to own the sleek new model **WHIZZER BROOMSTICK!**

Faster than a shooting star and smarter than the average broomstick with its go-faster lightning flashes, the Whizzer sells for **less** than the cost of a new robe and pointed hat – amazing!

Think how you would feel, the envy of all the other wizards, witches and warlocks, as you swept up to council meetings on a sporty new Whizzer. It's probably the best broomstick in the world!

Don't miss your chance to impress your friends with this unbeatable offer!

Task 2 Imagine you are writing an advertisement for Mugly and Bugly's Burp Juice – guaranteed to make your party go with a bang! Super! Here are some phrases to help you. You don't need to use them all.

Mugly & Bugly burp Juice

every right-thinking person
such a good deal
probably the best… in the world
all-time low price
how could you go wrong
no-one but a complete idiot

Task 3 Now, write a persuasive piece about why wizards need apprentices like you and me! I want Wizard Whimstaff to know we have thought about this carefully! Here are some ideas to get you started:

- Wizards need help around their caves to leave them free to do important things, like casting spells!
- There are so many potions in a wizard's cave that someone needs to organise them.
- They need someone to clean out the bats and spiders (and pet frogs!).
- Wizards need intelligent people to discuss their ideas with.

Sorcerer's Skill Check

Now, imagine you want a pet dragon. Write a passage to persuade your parents round to your way of thinking. Why should they buy you a dragon? It's easy when you know how!

Croak! We're convinced you should have a pet dragon! Have a silver shield for being so persuasive!

Intriguing Instructions

I'm Miss Snufflebeam.
I'm very forgetful so I write lots of **instructions**. Instructions tell people what to do. You sometimes find them on models that you are trying to make. Recipes are instructions too! Look at these instructions that Wizard Whimstaff wrote for washing my scales.

- Fetch a bucket of lukewarm water
- Add Dragon Scale Cleaner detergent
- Stir until water turns purple
- Add dragon
- Swish around until most of the water has sloshed over the side
- Remove dragon from suds and dry.

Task 1 Help! It's my turn to make lunch today and I don't want to forget! Write a set of clear instructions for me, about how to make a dragon scale sandwich. Don't forget to spread the bread with slime because dragon scales can be very dry on their own!

_____

_____

_____

_____

Task 2 I wrote out these instructions for riding a broomstick, but they seem to be in the wrong order! One of the most important things with instructions is getting the order right. Would you write it out again for me?

a Take one broomstick. _____

b Shout 'Down' when you fly too high. _____

c Say correct spell to ensure lift-off. _____

d Test it for flexibility and strength. _____

e Push off and pray. _____

f Place broomstick between legs. _____

Task 3

I'm just a small dragon and I'm not very scary! Dragons are supposed to be fierce. Can you write some instructions to help me to be frightening, like other dragons?

_____

_____

_____

_____

_____

_____

_____

_____

_____

Sorcerer's Skill Check

After all this thinking, my head hurts! I need to make a dessert for my lunch with Wizard Whimstaff. Write a recipe for chocolate crisp cakes, as they are his favourite food.

_____

_____

_____

_____

_____

You're a natural instructor! Give yourself a silver shield for your trophy!

Alarming Ambiguity

We're Mugly and Bugly, the lazy pet frogs! We like to confuse Pointy by saying things that are **ambiguous**, which is **when the meaning is not clear** because of the way the words are put together. Pointy is ambiguous too sometimes, but he doesn't mean to be!

> If that frog's not eating its food, throw it in the bin!

This sounds like someone wants to throw us away! We know that Pointy means the food, but it's still a disaster waiting to happen!

Task 1 Brain cell alert! Look at these advertisements from our local newspaper, then think about why they are ambiguous. What do they really mean?

Lost Black cat belonging to ten-year-old boy with a long furry tail and answering to the name of Neville.

For Sale Broomstick suitable for twelve-year-old girl in good condition.

Wanted Trick box for apprentice wizards young and old, silver or purple.

DANGER
Dead Slow Old People Crossing.

Task 2 Croak! Just to make sure we're on the right lines, could you correct these sentences? They sound a bit funny to us and we need a snooze.

a The boy we were looking for had new trousers with green glasses and ginger hair.

_____

b The girl asked a lady where to get off the bus wearing a pink hat.

_____

c The dragon lived in a lair next door to his best friend with very soft walls.

_____

d The goblin found the ring belonging to the lady made of gold.

_____

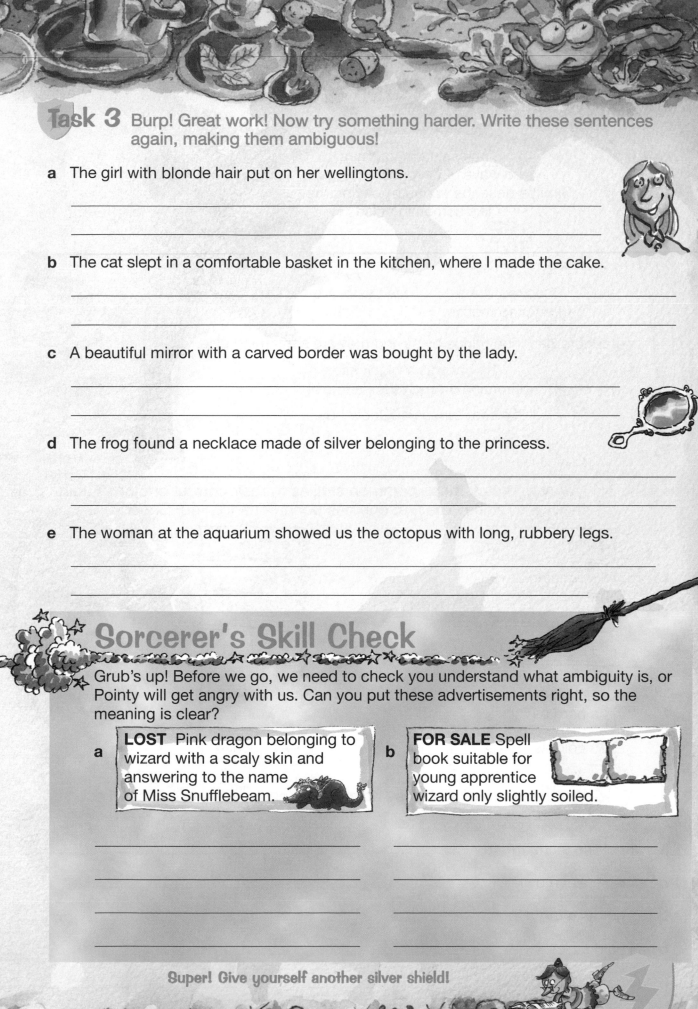

Task 3
Burp! Great work! Now try something harder. Write these sentences again, making them ambiguous!

a The girl with blonde hair put on her wellingtons.

_____
_____

b The cat slept in a comfortable basket in the kitchen, where I made the cake.

_____
_____

c A beautiful mirror with a carved border was bought by the lady.

_____
_____

d The frog found a necklace made of silver belonging to the princess.

_____
_____

e The woman at the aquarium showed us the octopus with long, rubbery legs.

_____
_____

Sorcerer's Skill Check

Grub's up! Before we go, we need to check you understand what ambiguity is, or Pointy will get angry with us. Can you put these advertisements right, so the meaning is clear?

a **LOST** Pink dragon belonging to wizard with a scaly skin and answering to the name of Miss Snufflebeam.

b **FOR SALE** Spell book suitable for young apprentice wizard only slightly soiled.

_____
_____
_____

Super! Give yourself another silver shield!

Similes and Metaphors

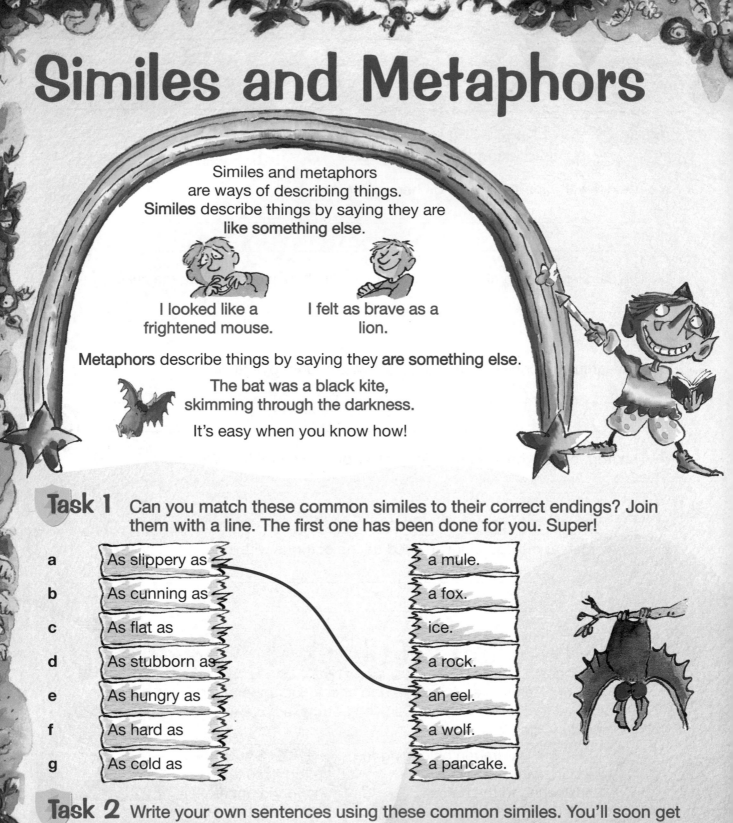

Similes and metaphors
are ways of describing things.
Similes describe things by saying they are
like something else.

I looked like a
frightened mouse.

I felt as brave as a
lion.

Metaphors describe things by saying they **are** something else.

The bat was a black kite,
skimming through the darkness.

It's easy when you know how!

Task 1 Can you match these common similes to their correct endings? Join
them with a line. The first one has been done for you. Super!

a As slippery as   a mule.

b As cunning as   a fox.

c As flat as   ice.

d As stubborn as   a rock.

e As hungry as   an eel.

f As hard as   a wolf.

g As cold as   a pancake.

Task 2 Write your own sentences using these common similes. You'll soon get
the hang of it!

a works like a charm   _____

b as wise as an owl   _____

c as hot as a furnace   _____

d as cold as ice   _____

e as dead as a doornail _____

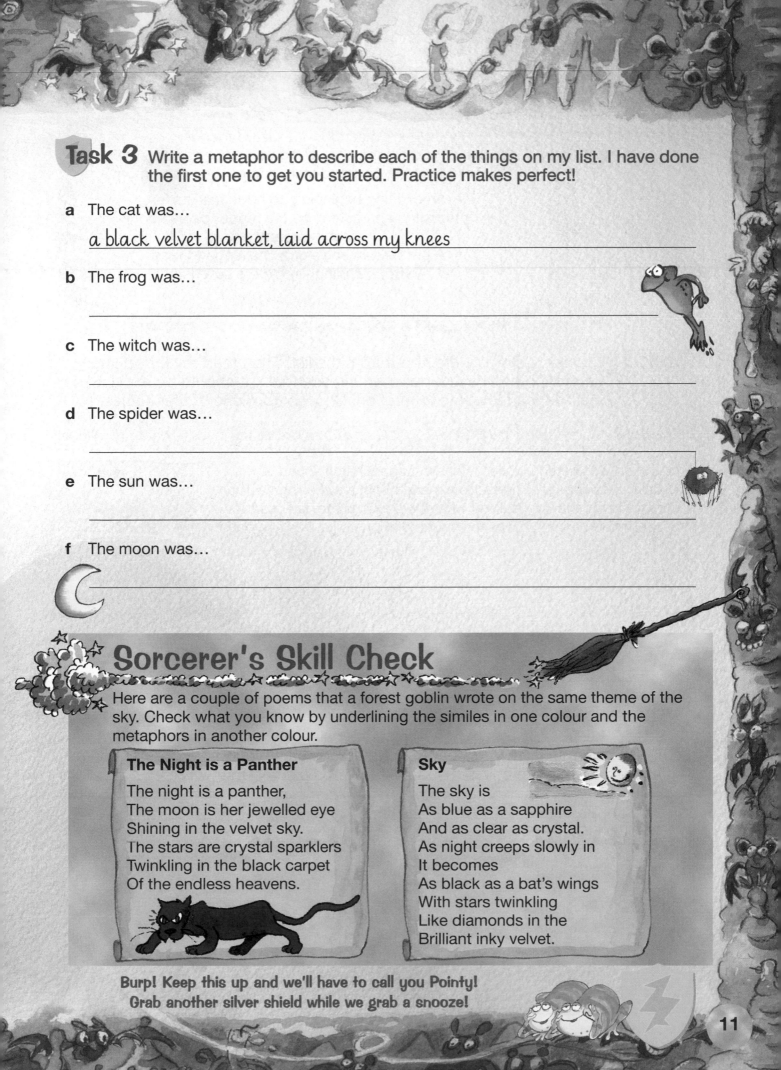

Task 3 Write a metaphor to describe each of the things on my list. I have done the first one to get you started. Practice makes perfect!

a The cat was…

a black velvet blanket, laid across my knees

b The frog was…

c The witch was…

d The spider was…

e The sun was…

f The moon was…

Sorcerer's Skill Check

Here are a couple of poems that a forest goblin wrote on the same theme of the sky. Check what you know by underlining the similes in one colour and the metaphors in another colour.

The Night is a Panther

The night is a panther,
The moon is her jewelled eye
Shining in the velvet sky.
The stars are crystal sparklers
Twinkling in the black carpet
Of the endless heavens.

Sky

The sky is
As blue as a sapphire
And as clear as crystal.
As night creeps slowly in
It becomes
As black as a bat's wings
With stars twinkling
Like diamonds in the
Brilliant inky velvet.

Burp! Keep this up and we'll have to call you Pointy!
Grab another silver shield while we grab a snooze!

Scary Stories

When I meet up with wizard friends, we spend many happy hours frightening one another with spooky tales! Every **good story** has things in common:

- An exciting beginning, to hook the reader
- Interesting characters, so the reader cares about what happens
- A problem to solve or a challenge to face
- A strong ending – maybe a surprise!

Hey Presto!

Task 1 Choose a title to write about from the list. Then read my introductory paragraph and have a go at writing your own. It should be exciting, so that the reader wants to read on! Choose from one of these titles.

The Echo	Creature of the Darkness	It Came From Under the Bed	The Empty House

The sound was getting closer. It was a ragged, harsh sound. A motorbike revving up? Thunder overhead? With a sickening flash of understanding, the boy realised what the sound in the dark, shadowy trees reminded him of. It was the sound of monstrous, heavy breathing.

_____

_____

_____

_____

_____

Task 2 Miss Snufflebeam has gone quite pale, as your introduction was so alarming! Now think about characters. I am writing a character outline for Jed, the boy in my story. Look at mine and then write your own.

Appearance: tall, thin. Dark hair and haunted eyes

Voice: low, speaks quietly

Clothes: jeans and black T shirt

Type of person: shy, quiet. Likes reading horror stories

Catchphrase: Amazing!

My Character

Appearance: _____

Voice: _____

Clothes: _____

Type of person: _____

Catchphrase: _____

Task 3

Now try to think of a problem or challenge for your character to face. Remember to include details about how your characters think and feel about the challenge or problem! Read my problem below, then work your own magic!

Jed meets an injured alien. It makes a link to him with its mind, so Jed knows it is not dangerous. But where will he hide his new friend from the mysterious armed troops that want to capture it?

Task 4

Excellent work! Now for a strong ending. Remember the ending must make sense but it can have an unexpected twist or surprise!

Jed walked slowly back down the hill. He had never felt so alone. Suddenly, a shooting star shot across the sky in front of him. His friend had gone, but would never be forgotten.

Sorcerer's Skill Check

It's time for you to magic up your own ideas, young apprentice! On a separate piece of paper, I want you to write a story about Jed discovering a magical land. You can have as many characters as you like. What adventures will Jed have? Who will he meet? What challenges will he face?

You're a splendid story writer! Have another shield!

Apprentice Wizard Challenge 1

Challenge 1 Think of some meaningful words to replace **nice** in these sentences!

a Flying through the air was such a nice experience. _____

b We saw a nice film about wonderful wizards. _____

c The magic marshmallow meringues were nice.  _____

d It's a change to see you looking so nice. _____

e Miss Snufflebeam is such a nice dragon. _____

f I hope the weather stays nice so we can bask by the pond. _____

g When we had finished the race, we had a nice drink of enchanted cola.

_____

Challenge 2 Imagine you are writing an advertisement for Miss Snufflebeam's favourite fire lighters, that help her to blow flames instead of puffs of smoke. Remember to be persuasive! Here are some phrases to help you. You do not need to use them all.

every right-thinking person
such a good deal
probably the best… in the world
all-time low price
how could you go wrong

_____
_____
_____
_____
_____
_____

Challenge 3 To check that you know exactly how to write instructions, write a list to tell someone how to make a cup of tea. Don't forget, it's important to get things in the right order!

_____
_____
_____
_____
_____

Challenge 4

Here are more ambiguous advertisements. Can you make the meaning clear by re-writing the sentences?

a **Lost:** Grey bat belonging to goblin with big flapping wings and answering to the name of Belfry.

_____
_____
_____

b **For Sale:** Cloak for a witch that is barely worn – just a bit frayed at the edges.

_____
_____
_____

c **Wanted:** Broomstick for elderly wizard that isn't too fast or sporty.

_____
_____
_____

Challenge 5

Look at these pairs of sentences. Tick the sentence that contains a simile and put a cross next to the sentence containing a metaphor.

a This pudding tastes like mud.

b This pudding is poison.

c He went like a bullet when he started the race.

d He was greased lightning in the Dragon Dash.

e Pointy was as cross as a wasp when he saw how little the frogs had done.

f Pointy exploded with anger when he realised they were asleep again.

Challenge 6

Write a story about a dragon on a separate piece of paper. Use the words below to give you some ideas. Don't forget to use a strong beginning and ending!

glittering   fierce   magical   serpent

scaly   shining   flames   roaring

Count how many challenges you got right and put stars on the test tube to show your score. Then have a silver shield for your trophy!

6

5

4

3

2

1

Challenge Score

Haunted Homophones

Homophones are words that sound alike but have **different spellings and meanings**. They can make spelling things quite tricky!

The words **which** and **witch** sound alike but their spellings and meanings are totally different.

Which cake shall I eat first?

The **witch** was very old.

You'll soon get the hang of it!

Task 1 There are two sets of homophones in the sentences below! Can you find them? There are three words in each set. Write them down and put the correct meaning.

I was discussing homophones with my two friends, Mugly and Bugly, but they're either too sleepy or too slow to catch on. Is there any point in explaining again? I really need their help, but it looks like you might have to come to my rescue!

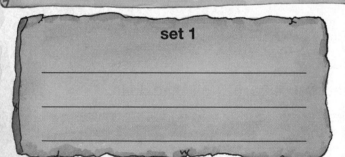

set 1

_____

_____

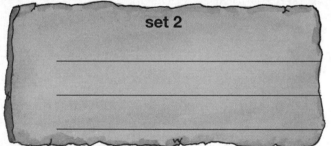

set 2

_____

_____

Task 2 Super start! Now use the words from the box to complete the exercise below. Write each word next to its homophone.

| wring | knot | whole | new | wrap | knight | piece | write | flour |

a peace _____

b knew _____

c flower _____

d ring _____

e hole _____

f rap _____

g night _____

h not _____

i right _____

Task 3 Practice makes perfect! Complete the short story below, choosing the correct homophone. I have given you a choice each time, so just choose one of the words in the brackets.

Last Saturday, I went to (meat, meet) _____ my friend, Miss Snufflebeam, in her cavern. When I got (there, they're, their) _____ , I noticed that she was looking a little (pail, pale) _____ . "I don't (no, know) _____ what's wrong with me," she said. "Maybe you (need, knead) _____ to take some dragon powder? I think I have some in my cave, unless I (through, threw) _____ it away," I said. "Let's go this (weigh, way) _____ . It's a little quicker." As we were walking to my cave, we (passed, past) _____ a wild (flour, flower) _____ stall and I stopped and bought (some, sum) _____ magic marigolds for Wizard Whimstaff. We reached the cave and I found the powder. I gave Miss S (two, to, too) _____ spoonfuls of powder immediately and suggested she take (two, to, too) _____ later (two, to, too) _____ . An (our, hour) _____ later she felt much better. That (night, knight) _____ I popped round to see the Wizard and gave him the marigolds. "You shouldn't (waist, waste) _____ your money on (presents, presence) _____ for me!" he said, but he was smiling! I (knew, new) _____ he was pleased. "That's okay Wizard Whimstaff. I wanted to (bye, buy) _____ them, but I wonder if I could have a (loan, lone) _____ because now I'm broke!" Before he had (thyme, time) _____ to reply, I had laughed and said, (Buy, Bye) "_____!".

Sorcerer's Skill Check

Now correct these sentences by circling the incorrectly used homophones. It's easy when you know how!

a By the time knight fell, I new the dragon would knot come.

b I would never have any piece until I new the hole magical story.

c The goblin spent an our righting down the spell.

d I could sea write threw the whole in the night's armour.

Brain cell alert! You're nearly as clever as Pointy! Give yourself another silver shield!

Creepy Comprehension

Comprehension means understanding and a **comprehension exercise** checks that you have understood the things you have read. Usually, you are asked to write answers to questions about a story or article. So in **comprehension tests**, it is important to read passages slowly and several times, if you don't understand the meaning at first.

Task 1 Read this magical passage carefully. Then read it again, making sure you understand what you have read.

I am the famous Wizard Whimstaff. Pointy has told me that my filing system is too old fashioned and I need to move into the 21st century. I agreed to buy a computer, so Pointy would be able to organise the cave and all my potions and spells more efficiently. While we were out shopping, Pointy also persuaded me to pick up an up-to-the-minute cloak with the latest designs of bats and toads! It has sparkling moondust sewn in, so my friends and I won't bump into each other when we're out on the broomsticks at night.

Several of my friends are now considering a similar change of style but I somehow think that the frogs, Mugly and Bugly, might be too idle to put any of them into practice. Miss Snufflebeam was contemplating changing her name to Snuffers to sound more trendy but I told her to keep her lovely name – it's much more dignified! I also told her that people might think that her fire-breathing had been permanently extinguished – 'snuffed out', even!

Task 2 Now answer the questions. Make sure you answer in full sentences. Abracadabra!

a Which century does Wizard Whimstaff need to move into?

_____

b Why did Pointy want Wizard Whimstaff to buy a computer?

_____

c What new item of clothing has the wizard bought?

_____

d Why does Miss Snufflebeam want to change her name?

_____

Task 3 Well done, young apprentice! Now write a paragraph either suggesting other ways to bring wizardry into the 21st century or giving reasons why it needs to be modernised.

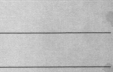

_____

_____

_____

_____

_____

_____

_____

_____

Sorcerer's Skill Check

Just to check that you have understood the passage you have read, answer these questions. Remember to use full sentences! Allakazan!

a Which characters are too lazy to change?

_____

b What new name is Miss Snufflebeam thinking about choosing?

_____

c Who bought a new cloak?

_____

d Who was keen to buy a new computer?

_____

e Explain the meaning of the word dignified.

_____

You soon got the hang of it! Give yourself another silver shield!

Lustrous Letters

I'm trying to write a **letter**.
Pointy says that to write letters you need to know the difference between **formal** and **informal** letter writing.

Formal letters are sent to people you don't know well and use formal language. They end in Yours sincerely.

Informal letters are sent to friends and family. You can write something in the same informal way that you would speak to them. Informal letters end in Best Wishes, or even Love!

You need to remember always to include your address at the top of the letter, so people can write back to you!

Task 1 I've been having trouble breathing flames, so I've written to the famous Dr. Dragon, asking for help. Unfortunately I've forgotten where to put the address and how to finish my letter. What do I say when it's a formal letter like this? Can you add the bits I've missed? My address is: Miss Snufflebeam, Wizard Whimstaff's Cave, Faraway Land.

_____

_____

_____

Dear Dr. Dragon,

I am writing to ask for your help. I am a young dragon and when I was little I had a nasty cough. The cough has gone, but now I can't breathe fire at all!

This is a great problem for me, as everyone believes that dragons are fierce and fiery. Nobody will take me seriously unless I can breathe fire and, if possible, roar and rumble.

Please tell me what to do.

_____

Miss Snufflebeam

Task 2 Oh dear! I can't wait for the reply! Write me a letter giving me ideas about how I can blow better flames – gargling with garlic juice, taking hot baths, chewing coal etc. Don't forget your address so I can write back to you!

Sorcerer's Skill Check

Mugly and Bugly gave me a big jar of squishy pondweed to soothe my throat. Can you test what you have learned and write them a thank you letter on your own writing paper?

Croak! What a great letter! Give yourself a silver shield!

21

Conjuring Conjunctions

I am here to help you with **conjunctions**. Conjunctions **connect sentences** and make them more interesting.

Words like **because, but, since, and, or, after, when, so, although** and **however**, can all be used to join two simple sentences to make one more interesting sentence.

I like toffees. I like fizzbombs.

These could be joined to make one more interesting sentence:

I like toffees and fizzbombs.

Task 1 Practice makes perfect! See if you can underline the conjunctions in these sentences.

a   I like sweets but I don't like chocolate.

b   I like Miss Snufflebeam and I like Pointy.

c   I wore my coat because it was raining.

d   I went to the beach although I don't like crabs!

e   I had a cool drink because it was a hot day.

f   The dragon jumped when she heard a loud noise.

Task 2 Wave your wand to join each pair of short sentences together with conjunctions.

a   I was wearing my warmest cloak _____ I started to shiver.

b   All frogs need water _____ they may dry up without it.

c   The sun came out _____ the ice began to thaw.

d   The sun came out _____ the day was still chilly.

e   Will the frogs be happy _____ will they be sad?

Task 3 Super work! Now try to do some of Mugly and Bugly's more complicated sentences. You may find you need to use commas as well. Try using **when, because, although, before, but**. Remember, don't ever use **but** at the beginning of a sentence!

When two or more sentences repeat some of the same information, you can combine them into one sentence using fewer words.

a Croak! I woke up. I ate 8 flies. I am listening to my disc player.

Croak! I woke up, ate 8 flies and am now listening to my disc player.

b The sun came out. The river started to thaw. The pond also thawed.

_____

_____

c I talked to my plants. I watered them every day. They still died.

_____

_____

d The rain continued for days. The river flooded. It threatened to cover the roads.

_____

_____

Sorcerer's Skill Check

For your final conjunction conjuring trick, can you do these tasks? It's easy when you know how!

a Why do we use conjunctions?

_____

_____

_____

b Put a circle around all the words in the box that are conjunctions.

because   dragon   but   I   since   spell   water   and   after

sweets   cold   when   so   although   pumpkin   however

You're a natural conjurer! Add a silver shield to your trophy!

Magical Haiku

Croak! We're excited! We have just discovered that we can write Japanese poetry! And we can't even speak Japanese! We like **Haiku** poems because they are very short, which leaves more time for snoozing! Each poem has **3 lines**, made up of **17 syllables**.

The first line has <u>5</u> syllables.
The second line has <u>7</u> syllables.
The third line has <u>5</u> syllables.

My favourite frog
Loves to laze in the lovely
Afternoon sunshine

Haiku use lots of **alliteration**, which means **using the same letter more than once,** so it sounds poetic.

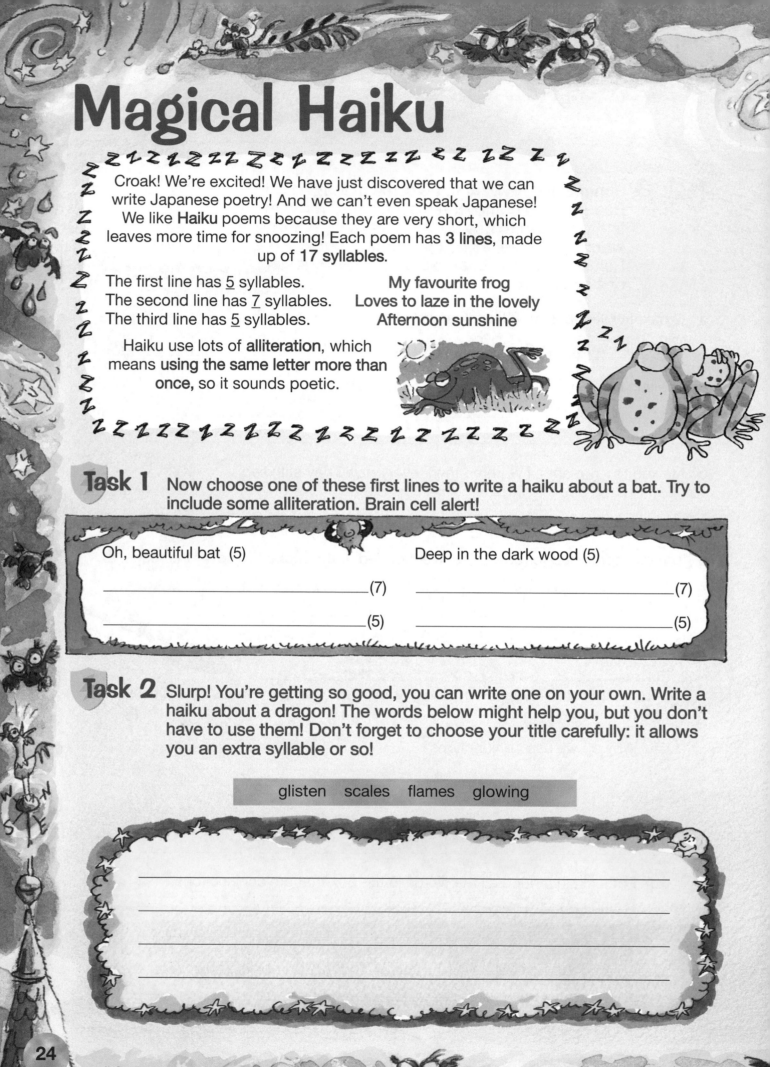

Task 1

Now choose one of these first lines to write a haiku about a bat. Try to include some alliteration. Brain cell alert!

Oh, beautiful bat (5)

_____ (7)

_____ (5)

Deep in the dark wood (5)

_____ (7)

_____ (5)

Task 2

Slurp! You're getting so good, you can write one on your own. Write a haiku about a dragon! The words below might help you, but you don't have to use them! Don't forget to choose your title carefully: it allows you an extra syllable or so!

glisten   scales   flames   glowing

_____

_____

_____

_____

Task 3 To write a haiku, you need to know about syllables. Some people clap the syllables, but Mugly and I like to burp ours! Mark this haiku into syllables. The first line has been done for you. Then write another haiku and mark it into syllables. Hope you're good at burping!

> Bats, / bugs / and / oth / er
> Creepy crawly creatures love
> To meet at midnight

Sorcerer's Skill Check

We're getting hungry now, so write a haiku about our favourite food: bugs, slugs and crispy spiders! Yum! Don't forget to give it a title!

What a great dragon haiku you wrote! Give yourself a silver shield!

First and Third Person

Oh dear! Wizard Whimstaff has asked me to explain the difference between writing in the **first person** and writing in the **third person**.

When you **write about yourself**, you write in the **first person**.

I am a small dragon who lives in a magical cave with Wizard Whimstaff.

When you write in the **third person**, you **write about someone else**. Look at this article about Wizard Whimstaff that Pointy wrote for Wizard's World magazine.

Wizard Whimstaff is a well known wizard currently living in a large, magical cave in a dark forest. He rides a very sporty broomstick and has been known to exceed the speed limit! Whimstaff is a brilliant sorcerer and is terrifically talented at teaching children to improve their English.

Task 1 I find this all rather hard! Let's see if you're cleverer than I am. Change the article about Wizard Whimstaff from the third person to the first person. Imagine that you are Wizard Whimstaff himself!

Task 2 You are clever! Now read this piece I wrote, describing myself to my penfriend. I wrote it in the first person. On a separate piece of paper, rewrite my work in the third person, using **she** and **her** instead of **I** and **me**.

I'm Miss Snufflebeam. I'm a very small and rather timid dragon. I'm lucky to have a good friend called Wizard Whimstaff, who makes me feel quite special. I'm rather shy and I have great trouble breathing fire, which does not make me a very scary dragon! I would like to be able to breathe fire and roar in a terrifying way!

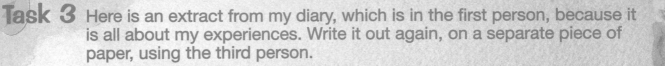

Task 3 Here is an extract from my diary, which is in the first person, because it is all about my experiences. Write it out again, on a separate piece of paper, using the third person.

Tuesday 13 March

Today I was lucky. I found a shiny scale on the way to Fire Breathing Classes. I think it must have fallen out of someone's pocket because it had little pieces of gold attached to it. I took it to the school office and the chief goblin told me that if nobody claimed it, I could have it at 3.30. Finally 3.30 arrived. I felt nervous when I went into the office. The secretary smiled at me and handed me the scale, saying that nobody had claimed it. On the way home I bought a magazine called Dangerous Dragon.

Task 4 Now write a part of a diary about yourself, on a separate piece of paper. Write about a time between coming home from school and going to bed. It will all have to be in the first person!

Sorcerer's Skill Check

I'm still a bit confused. Mark these sentences to show if they are third person (3) or first person (1)

a Pointy went to the shop.

b I love puffing smoke!

c I went to the cinema to see a film about a young wizard. It was great!

d Mugly burps a lot.

e Wizard Whimstaff is very clever.

f Miss Snufflebeam is pink and shiny.

Well done, young apprentice! You have really helped Miss Snufflebeam. Take another silver shield for your trophy!

Apprentice Wizard Challenge 2

Challenge 1
Underline the homophone pairs in these sentences.

a The cats ate their fish, then sat over there.

b The wizard could not undo the knot.

c Pointy would get no peace until he gave Mugly and Bugly a piece of cake.

d I must wrap the rap CD I have bought for my brother's birthday.

e The knight ran off into the night.

Challenge 2
Read the passage and answer the questions. Remember to use full sentences!

> Wizard Whimstaff has two pet frogs called Mugly and Bugly. Some of their habits are disgusting! They burp and slurp all day! They are rather lazy but try to help before they drop off for another snooze! Miss Snufflebeam, the little pink dragon, is rather absent-minded, but she tries to be as helpful as possible!

a What are Wizard Whimstaff's pets called?

_____

b What sort of animals are they?

_____

c What bad habits do they have?

_____

d What does absent–minded mean?

_____

Challenge 3
Wizard Whimstaff needs to write a formal letter to the Wizards' Council telling them about a new potion he has invented. What does the potion do? Why is he excited? On a separate piece of paper write the letter for him, setting out the address correctly and starting and finishing the letter in a formal way.

Challenge 4 Choose the best conjunction for the following sentences.

a Don't fly off _____ all the dragons are here.

b She is absent _____ a wizard put a spell on her.

c Mugly is a lazy frog _____ Bugly is even lazier.

d _____ your spell-making improves, I won't give you any pocket money.

e Gimble is a good goblin _____ Pointy is even better.

f _____ he had been forbidden to do so, he went to the magic pond at midnight.

Challenge 5 Write a haiku about casting spells. Use some of the words on the potion bottles to help you, but you don't need to use them all!

_____

_____

_____

_____

bang

stink

flash

ogre

gas

sparks   wand

Challenge 6 Change these sentences from first person to third person.

a I am going to change myself into a handsome prince.

_____

_____

b I was on my way to the apprentice class when I realised that I had left my wand behind.

_____

_____

c I wanted to learn how to fly so I asked the dragon to teach me.

_____

_____

Count how many challenges you got right and put stars on the test tube to show your score. Then take the last silver shield for your trophy!

6

5

4

3

2

Challenge Score

Answers

Pages 2–3

Task 1 Many answers are possible.
Suggestions are:

a sunny	**e** lovely
b bubbling	**f** yummy
c fun	**g** friendly
d gleaming	**h** powerful

Task 2 Many answers are possible.
Suggestions are:

a evil	**e** boring
b dreadful	**f** tragic
c weak	**g** dirty
d silly	**h** terrifying

Task 3 Many answers are possible.

Sorcerer's Skill Check
Many answers are possible.

Pages 4–5

Task 1 Persuasive language is:
be the first, sleek new model,
Faster, smarter, sells for less,
amazing, envy, sporty, new,
probably the best broomstick in the
world, Don't miss your chance,
impress your friends,
unbeatable offer.

Task 2 Many answers are possible.

Task 3 Many answers are possible.

Sorcerer's Skill Check
Many answers are possible.

Pages 6–7

Task 1 Many answers are possible.
An example answer would be:
Take some fresh dragon scales.
Chop them into small pieces.
Take two pieces of brown bread.
Spread them with snail slime.
Arrange dragon scales in bread.
Chop sandwich in half and eat.

Task 2 Take one broomstick. **a**
Test it for flexibility and strength. **d**
Place broomstick between legs. **f**
Say correct spell to ensure lift-off. **c**
Push off and pray. **e**
Shout 'Down' when you fly too high. **b**

Task 3 Many answers are possible.

Sorcerer's Skill Check
Many answers are possible.
An example is:
Melt some margarine in a
saucepan.
Stir in some sugar, golden syrup
and cocoa powder.
Add cornflakes and mix well.
Spoon the mixture into small paper
cases.
Leave to cool.

Pages 8–9

Task 1 A boy has lost a cat called Neville
with a long furry tail.
A girl needs a broomstick in good
condition.
Apprentice wizards young and old
require a trick box, silver or purple.
Go very slowly as old people are
crossing.

Task 2 **a** The boy we were looking for had
green glasses, ginger hair and
new trousers.
b The girl asked a lady wearing a
pink hat where to get off the bus.
c The dragon lived in a lair with very
soft walls next door to his best
friend.
d The goblin found the ring made of
gold belonging to the lady.

Task 3 **a** The girl put on her wellingtons
with blonde hair.
b The cat slept in the kitchen in a
comfortable basket where I made
the cake.
c A beautiful mirror was bought by
the lady with a carved border.
d The frog found a necklace
belonging to the princess made of
silver.
e The woman showed us the
octopus at the aquarium with
long, rubbery legs.

Sorcerer's Skill Check
a LOST Pink dragon with a scaly
skin answering to the name of
Miss Snufflebeam belonging to a
wizard.
b FOR SALE Spell book only
slightly soiled suitable for young
apprentice wizard.

Pages 10–11

Task 1 **a** As slippery as an eel.
b As cunning as a fox.
c As flat as a pancake.
d As stubborn as a mule.
e As hungry as a wolf.
f As hard as a rock.
g As cold as ice.

Task 2 Many answers are possible.

Task 3 Many answers are possible.

Sorcerer's Skill Check
The following words should be
underlined:
Similes: blue as a sapphire, clear as
crystal, black as a bat's wings,
twinkling like diamonds.
Metaphors: a panther, jewelled eye,
velvet sky, crystal sparklers, black
carpet.

Pages 12–13

Task 1 Many answers are possible.

Task 2 Many answers are possible.

Task 3 Many answers are possible.

Task 4 Many answers are possible.

Sorcerer's Skill Check
Many answers are possible.

Pages 14–15

Challenge 1
Many answers are possible.
Some suggestions are:
a fantastic
b exciting
c delicious
d elegant
e happy
f lovely
g refreshing

Challenge 2
Many answers are possible.

Challenge 3
Variations on the following are
acceptable:
First, boil the kettle.
Put a teabag in a cup.
When the kettle has boiled, add
water to the cup.
Remove the teabag after it has
brewed.
Add milk and sugar as needed.

Challenge 4
a Lost: A grey bat with big flapping
wings and answering to the name
of Belfry, belonging to a goblin.
b A witch's cloak barely worn – just
a bit frayed at the edges – is for
sale.
c Wanted: A broomstick that isn't
too fast or sporty for an elderly
wizard.

Challenge 5

a tick	**d** cross
b cross	**e** tick
c tick	**f** cross

Challenge 6
Many answers are possible.

Pages 16–17

Task 1 The two sets are:
set 1
they're – they are
there – used as a grammatical
subject with some verbs
their – belonging to them
set 2
to – to mark the infinitive of a verb
two – number after one
too – more than you want.

Task 2 **a** peace, piece
b knew, new
c flower, flour
d ring, wring
e hole, whole
f rap, wrap
g night, knight
h not, knot
i right, write

Task 3 Last Saturday, I went to <u>meet</u> my
friend, Miss Snufflebeam, in her
cavern. When I got <u>there</u>, I noticed
that she was looking a little <u>pale</u>. "I
don't <u>know</u> what's wrong with me,"
she said. "Maybe you <u>need</u> to take
some dragon powder? I think I have
some in my cave, unless I <u>threw</u> it
away," I said. "Let's go this <u>way</u>. It's
a little quicker." As were walking to
my cave, we <u>passed</u> a wild <u>flower</u>
stall and I stopped and bought
<u>some</u> magic marigolds for Wizard
Whimstaff. We reached the cave
and I found the powder. I gave Miss
S <u>two</u> spoonfuls of powder
immediately and suggested she
take <u>two</u> later <u>too</u>. An <u>hour</u> later she
felt much better. That <u>night</u> I
popped round to see the Wizard
and gave him the marigolds. "You
shouldn't <u>waste</u> your money on

presents for me!" he said, but he was smiling! I <u>knew</u> he was pleased. "That's okay Wizard Whimstaff. I wanted to <u>buy</u> them, but I wonder if I could have a <u>loan</u> because now I'm broke!" Before he had <u>time</u> to reply, I had laughed and said, "<u>Bye</u>!".

Sorcerer's Skill Check

  a by the time (knight) fell, I (new) the dragon would (knot) come.

  b I would never have any (piece) until I (new) the (hole) magical story.

  c The goblin spent an (our) (righting) down the spell.

  d I could (sea) (write) (threw) the (whole) in the (night's) (armour).

Pages 18–19

Task 2 a Wizard Whimstaff needs to move into the 21st century.

  b Pointy wants Wizard Whimstaff to buy a computer to organise the cave and all his potions and spells more efficiently.

  c The wizard has bought an up-to the-minute cloak.

  d Miss Snufflebeam wants to change her name to sound more trendy.

Task 3 Many answers are possible.

Task 4 a Mugly and Bugly are too lazy to change.

  b She is thinking of choosing Snuffers.

  c Wizard Whimstaff bought a new cloak.

  d Pointy wanted to buy a new computer.

  e Dignified means important or distinctive. (Variations are acceptable.)

Pages 20–21

Task 1 Miss Snufflebeam's address should be in the top right-hand corner and Yours sincerely should be at the bottom of the letter.

Task 2 Many answers are possible. Address should be at the top right-hand corner and Yours sincerely/best wishes/love should be at the bottom of the letter.

Sorcerer's Skill Check
Many answers are possible.

Pages 22–23

Task 1 a I like sweets <u>but</u> I don't like chocolate.

  b I like Miss Snufflebeam <u>and</u> I like Pointy.

  c I wore my coat <u>because</u> it was raining.

  d I went to the beach <u>although</u> I don't like crabs.

  e I had a cool drink <u>because</u> it was a hot day.

  f The dragon jumped <u>when</u> she heard a loud noise.

Task 2 a Possible answers are: because, since, but, however.

  b Possible answers are: because, and, as.

  c Possible answers are: so, and.

  d Possible answers are: although, but.

  e or

Task 3 Many answers are possible. The following are examples only.

  a Croak! I woke up, ate 8 flies and am now listening to my disc player.

  b The sun came out, the river started to thaw and the pond also thawed.

  c I talked to my plants and I watered them every day, but they still died.

  d The rain continued for days before the river flooded and it threatened to cover the roads.

Sorcerer's Skill Check

  a An example answer would be: We use conjunctions to join sentences and make our writing more interesting.

  b The conjunctions are: because, but, since, and, after, when, so, although, however.

Pages 24–25

Task 1 Many answers are possible. Each haiku should have three lines with syllables of 5,7,5.

Task 2 Many answers are possible.

Task 3 Bats,/bugs/and/oth/er Creep/y/craw/ly/crea/tures/love To/meet/at/mid/night

Sorcerer's Skill Check
Many answers are possible.

Pages 26–27

Task 1 I'm a well known wizard currently living in a large, magical cave in a dark forest. I ride a very sporty broomstick and have been known to exceed the speed limit! I'm a brilliant sorcerer and I'm terrifically talented at teaching children to improve their English.

Task 2 She's Miss Snufflebeam. She's a very small and rather timid dragon. She's lucky to have a good friend called Wizard Whimstaff, who makes her feel quite special. She's rather shy and she has great trouble breathing fire, which does not make her a very scary dragon! She would like to be able to breathe fire and roar in a terrifying way!

Task 3 Tuesday she was lucky. She found a shiny scale on the way to Fire Breathing Classes. She thinks it must have fallen out of someone's pocket because it had little pieces of gold attached to it. She took it to the school office and the chief goblin told her that if nobody claimed it, she could have it at 3.30. Finally 3.30 arrived. She felt nervous when she went into the office. The secretary smiled at her and handed her the scale, saying that nobody had claimed it. On the way home she bought a magazine called Dangerous Dragon.

Task 4 Many answers are possible.

Sorcerer's Skill Check

a 3	**d** 3
b 1	**e** 3
c 1	**f** 3

Pages 28–29

Challenge 1

  a their, there

  b not, knot

  c peace, piece

  d wrap, rap

  e knight, night

Challenge 2

  a They are called Mugly and Bugly.

  b They are frogs.

  c They burp, slurp and are lazy.

  d It means forgetful.

Challenge 3
Many answers are possible. The address should be at the top right-hand side of the page and the letter should end Yours sincerely.

Challenge 4

  a Possible answers are: because, as, when

  b Possible answers are: as, because, after

  c Possible answers are: however, but

  d until

  e Possible answers are: but, however

  f although

Challenge 5
Many answers are possible. The haiku should have three lines with syllables of 5, 7, 5.

Challenge 6

  a He was going to change himself into a handsome prince.

  b He/she was on the way to the apprentice class when he/she realised that he/she had left his/her wand behind.

  c He/she wanted to learn how to fly so he/she asked the dragon to teach him/her.

The end

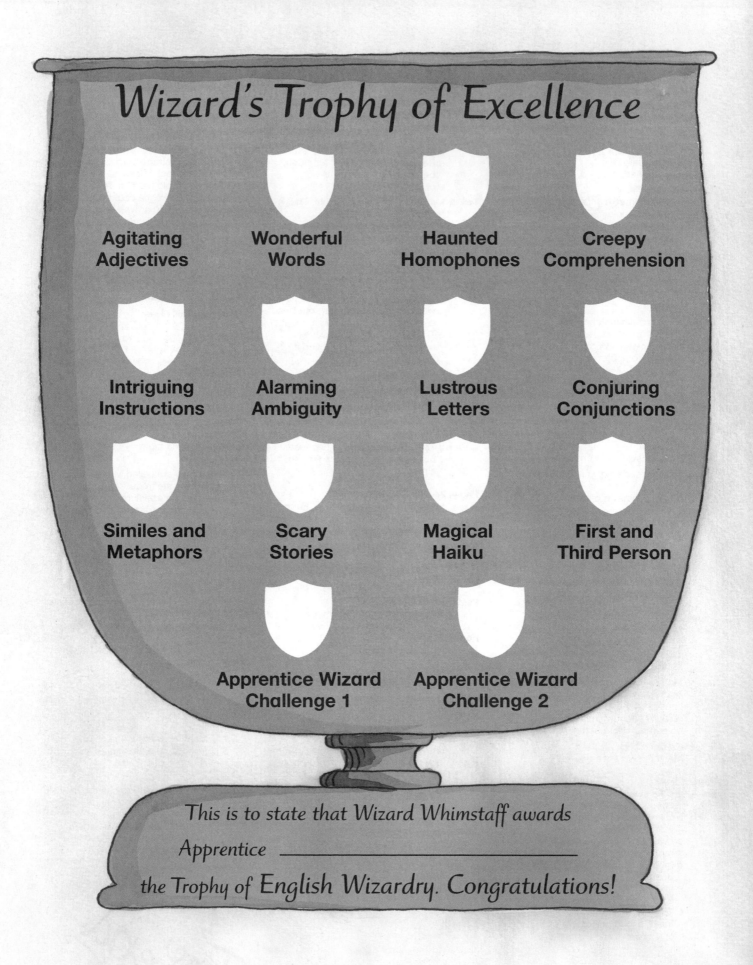